life.
love.
other.

Ben Wilson is a journalist and former editor of *Official PlayStation Magazine* and a number of successful websites. He was born in South London and now lives near Bath, juggling the responsibilities of being a single parent with freelance writing commitments. His work has featured in *The Guardian*, *The Telegraph*, *The Independent*, and many more. Wilson's debut book, *One Year Without Social Media*, was published in 2021 to strong reviews. This is his first poetry collection.

life.
love.
other.

BEN WILSON

LIFE. LOVE. OTHER.

Copyright © 2023 Ben Wilson

First published in Great Britain by KDP 2023

All rights reserved

Ben Wilson has asserted his right under the Copyright, Designs and Patent Acts 1988 to be identified as the author of this work.

No part of this book may be reproduced, or stored in a retrieval system, or transmitted in any form or by any means, electronic, mechanical, photocopying, recording, or otherwise, without express written permission of the publisher. Under no circumstances may any part of this book be photocopied for resale.

ISBN-13: 9798851405785

Cover design by Andrew Leung
Cover illustration by Scarlett Wilson

For Sarah-May
For our Tuesdays

life. love. other.

Contents

Mow	9
Ramsden	10
The Fear	11
Posters	12
September	13
Holding Hands	14
Amazonian	15
Day Trip	16
Rain	18
New Job	19
Coast	20
Moon	21
Stickers	22
Daybreak	23
Modern Dating	24
Seashell	27
Time	28
Sheets	29
Life Is In Pain	30
Regrets	31
Dreams	32
End	33
Postcard	34
Love In Age	36
Toothbrush	37
Keep Going	38
Ashtray	39
Meanwhile	40
Wind	41
Little Things	42
Somer	44
You And Me, Kid	45
Train	46

life. love. other.

Mow

What made me cut the grass?
Surrounded by closed doors,
Outside in name only.
But then
A ping, an opening.
A window and an invite.
A sweet escape, a new start?
Freedom.
Yours, mine, ours.
Barefoot in summer,
Sandal-clad in spring,
"I'm your girl for all seasons," she says,
As locks unlatch and walls crumble.
Gardening of a different kind.
Roses,
Kisses,
Honey blossom,
Happy.

Ben Wilson

Ramsden

The white van sitting at
The red light, or the blue
Jacket keeping the cyclist
Warm. Black numbers on

The scuffed town hall door,
Amber indicators signifying
The turning of a corner -
These are the colours

Of life, washed into
A sea of urbanity,
Viewed through new windows
On a stucco grey eve.

life. love. other.

The Fear

9am blue sky
With summer sun lies.
Blush, don't blush.
Backstage romance –
Keep the hush,
Don't leave to chance

9pm darkness
With limelight moon breaths.
Cry, don't cry.
I'm here for you –
Wipe your eyes,
I'm frightened too.

Posters

Half-dried Blu Tack
Holds craggy ends
Of old paper,
Forgotten friends

In photos on
A brown wardrobe:
Deleted songs,
Retired shows.

The tickets line
These cream-green walls –
A wafer shield
To constant calls

From time to move
Away from pasts.
All these asides
Will leave to last

My blank reprieve
Masking the gloom:
The posters which
Adorn this room.

life. love. other.

September

Under the damp bus shelter
He stands and waits
As time ticks
And ticks again.

From the crimson-walled kitchen
She sees the sun
Kiss horizon;
Long sobs in pain.

The patio lamp needs fixing –
Still as was left.
No more light
Through evening rain.

Ben Wilson

Holding Hands

Again, again,
You smile, you grin.
I feel your smile within, within.

Where have we been, where do we go?
Will we be here one year from now?

A lost foothole, a lifeless aim,
A lull in time, an endless game?

I feel your smile within, within.
Again, again,
You smile, you grin.

life. love. other.

Amazonian

I love the way you wear your
Collar up and your guard down.
Turn away and keep me waiting
For you to come, twice at once,
Like buses in the evening rush,

With purple skies that dance and glow
As if lavender fields aflame.
A rainforest-like confusion
Where all trees are forbidden love
And hate falls, like hail, from above.

Ben Wilson

Day Trip

Ice cream cones, razor pebbles, lads
Kicking seaweed and slinging sand –
Features of this September fad
Where my shoulders are burned by bland

Sunshine. Parents head for the shops
While little brothers scream, and fight,
And mini-Swift in low-cut top
Helps her sister to fly a kite,

Watched avidly by a deckchair
Veteran. The waves roll on, rush in
As sleep descends with fresh salt air.
This is the part where seagulls sing –

Except the slumber brings no rest,
No poet's dreams. Instead, the sea
Turns back to France, the sun heads west
With this relaxed monotony

In hand. A picnic by the pier,
A last barefoot game of cricket
And summer fades for one more year
To Littlehampton at sunset.

life. love. other.

Through the back window of the car
We watch the waves bounce off the groynes
While bloke with metal detector
Searches out scraps and ten pence coins.

Rain

I love the rain.

We walk through it,
kiss as the water runs
between our noses.

You thread your fingers
through my soaked hair;
When we get in, we'll

remove each other's clothing,
hang ourselves out to dry,
radiate together.

I love the rain.

life. love. other.

New Job

Lost telephone calls.
Whispered double-glazing
Voices cracking air.
Jackknifing the boredom

With thoughts of tomorrow:
The sight of your smile
As we stroll to work.
It makes it worthwhile.

Ben Wilson

Coast

Soft morning ocean breeze sighs
Another summer's day,
Watching strepitous seagulls
Bicker across the bay.
The reggae soldier's boombox
Plays one more sunshine song,
Simple plans for this evening:
Alcoholic and long.

How I wish you were here too
Stroking my sunburnt skin,
Sharing lingering kisses
As nightfall shimmers in.
I love the twilight coastline
But that's the conch I crave:
Your sweet smile pressed unto mine
In rhythm with the waves.

life. love. other.

Moon

Soft, silent, weak,
Lying so still
In stone motion.
Sand and ocean
Beg you to speak,

Flagging your white
Lost face in space.
You hold our past
Lives safe; dreams cast
Shadows on time.

Ben Wilson

Stickers

Got, got, got, got, got, got, got, need!
Sorting until your fingers bleed
On gravel playgrounds, rain or shine:
Those foil badges must be mine.
And even now lost eighties names
Are etched upon this greying brain,
All thanks to my Panini fix:
Still love you, Steve Ogrizovic.

There's just no joy in life quite like
Arriving home by mountain bike
To seal that final sticker in.
Grabbing your album with a grin,
Hurrying to the fateful page –
To see glee swapped for endless rage
'Cause in the haste of break time fun
You nabbed #19, not #91.

Daybreak

The rose dawn brings dew,
Gleaming like our dream future.
Love. Just me and you.

Modern Dating

Those
Rosebud
Early
Days.
Breathless,
Limitless.
Swipe,
Smile.
Yes?
Yes!

The meet-cute –
All bluebells
And butterflies.
First kisses,
First times.
Cold evenings,
Huddled hugs,
Hot flushes
Against the
Shower wall.

The middle act:
The daisy days,

life. love. other.

The Netflix nights.
The questions rise.
But do you?
I don't know.
Can we wait?
There's no time.
One shared bond,
Two different worlds.

The first few fissures,
Proud peonies wilting away.
Cracks in the tiling
Where you felt sure-footed.
But I thought that –
But you never asked.
I shouldn't have to.
From fears to tears.
Holding on, holding on,
Knowing you're losing grip.

The bursting of the banks.
White lilies and endless regret.
Conversations drawn out and strained,
A circle line of discontent.
Yet still the love overwhelms.
Don't end it? Stay friends?

Ben Wilson

There is no easy answer
So you question, again and
Again and again and again.
Until there is no more.

Together you sob, swear, subside.
Carnations, commiserations. Platonic pledges.
Until the words
Dry up.
Done.

life. love. other.

Seashell

The tears
Wish you back
Every day
  While
The fears
Leave memories
Washed away.

Time

Threadbare evenings passing
In Sussex sunset,
Devon beaches whispering

Days away – unprinted obituaries
Never to be reread,
Just blank colourless pages

Like the rest of the past:
Nothing in the end.
Only sleep, and a headstone,

And a small patch of grass.

Sheets

Started sleeping
On your side of the bed
To fill the void
From when you left.
But this, but this
Was always the issue:
So simpatico
Yet incompatible.
Different indents, lives.
I'm stealing your pillow
And I can hear you
Chastising me
And though I don't fit,
Though we never fit,
I wish, I wish,
You were doing it for real.

Life Is In Pain

Life is in pain. It screams and scowls and groans,
Encased in the glow of forgotten friends
Who etch your mind with both their smiles and moans.
We wither when we have to make our ends,
Allow our hearts to be cast into stone –

Joyous cries are echoes from summers past,
Relationships that splintered at the seams
Then slipped from the clifftop, spiralling fast,
Alongside all our crumbled childhood dreams.
Life is in pain if you're not first. I'm last.

life. love. other.

Regrets

Slowly, they seep in.
Deep in my stomach,
Like spiders creeping
Down my throat.
Last rites in weeping.

Dreams

On our balcony
Stands a chair. Sometimes,
I laze out there and
Search myself for bright dreams.

In our small kitchen
Lies a table. Dreams
Sit around it when
They have nowhere to go.

In the chamber, my
Bed entices sleep.
Black nightmares forbid –
So dreams relax elsewhere.

Inside our bathroom,
Dreams wash themselves
Using the sink. I am,
I think, too stale for them.

life. love. other.

End

Words are so sad
But there are none
For how I feel
Now that you're gone.

Ben Wilson

Postcard

A rainbow of flowers stands
opposite the hotel; the wind
dragging one corner of the
plastic-sleeved farewell back
across itself. The dislodged bricks,
marked by the accident, rest
ignorant, gawping at cliffs
and sea reaching its mute horizon.

I walk towards the Western pier,
eyes fixed on its blue head.
It juts into the waves, forming
a counterfeit symbol of life;
maybe the only one in this
desolate seaside town. Starboard
the old boys' pub sits closed,
while a sparse gathering of

tins-on-wheels spans a featureless
car park. A stream of banality
flows, shambolic nothingness
corrupted in a chain of thought.
Yet February will soon fade,
carrying tranquillity from boredom,

life. love. other.

transmogrifying fear to hope.
So the pensioners on benches

and the stale stag-do students
wait for a barrage of soles to
stomp sand onto the pier.
For coloured trees, full NCPs.
Days when, amid a summer of smiles,
the flowers will lie, dry, forgotten,
the plastic torn, ink smudged,
a lost last ode to someone special.

Love In Age

Days stand still –
Dead as night;
Words run stained
From the page.

Welcomes pass
No through road,
Last encore
Leaves the stage.

Time capsule
Clasps the past:
Broken hearts,
Bitter rage,

Album shots
Faded grey –
Symbols of
Love in age.

life. love. other.

Toothbrush

Poor fallow thing,
Standing on end,
Ruffled above the shoulders.

You help us smile;
Yet in your loneliness,
You never smile yourself.

Ben Wilson

Keep Going

It's over now. You can not breathe.
Salty tears moisten your sleeve.
The inner burning makes you heave.
Keep going, keep going, keep going.

Suffocated by hurt and heat.
Oceans of sweat, war gun heartbeat.
Limp shoulders pinned against the sheets.
Keep going, keep going, keep going.

Lungs constricted by the dawn crush.
Mind of jelly, limbs turned to mush.
Brain detonating in the hush.
Keep going, keep going, keep going.

It was not you. *It is not you.*
Stop turning red flags into blue.
Hijack the lies, embrace the true.
Keep going, keep going, keep going.

And take my word, this is no end.
Please call your family. Text a friend.
I swear, I swear that you will mend.
Keep going, keep going, keep going.

Ashtray

It only takes two minutes.
A little time and effort –
But it can be won.
Cleansing the system
For tomorrow, spun

Into orbit at no peril.
Map the wounds, form
A universe undone.
Fresh as a clean ashtray.
You'll learn one day, son.

Ben Wilson

Meanwhile

High chair, cramped table, tulips in a vase:
The least likely workplace in all mankind.
But how I love this secret world of ours,
The lunchtime insights into your sweet mind.

The garden left unmowed and overgrown,
Slowly becoming my new favourite view.
Blue fence, green grass, red truck parked all alone
Awaiting tiny hands in summers new.

Pattering words, shared post-code anecdotes,
Chocolate wrappers, guts full of too much tea,
Platonic laughs… wait, darling, grab your coat!
We'd better get the kids, it's five to three.

And as I read this back to you I know
There'll be some tears, a cringe, a little smile –
But best human, I just needed to show
I've got your back for aeons past meanwhile.

life. love. other.

Wind

Farting in bed:
"I hate it," she said.
"Do that once more
And you will be dead."

And so here I lie
The day after I died
Thanks to one unplanned blast
As I turned on my side.

Little Things

Is this why it always crumbles?
I'm not one for
Surprise trips to sunshine climes,
Bank note flourishes or credit card chimes.
Planting love bombs beneath burning bridges,
Or photos juxtaposed
To prove our compatibility on social media.
Am I doing it wrong?

I hope not.
For me, it's the little things.
A soft kiss before I pour you a drink.
A warm hug when you've had a bad day.
Train journeys learning your best mate's best song
So I can serenade you both with a voice note.
Substance over style,
Hoping that's enough for a while.

Walks by the weir,
Arcade games on the pier.
Cuddles and whispers in the garden in the dark,
Spoon-shaped mornings setting fire to our spark.
Moments that can't be captured for Facebook or Insta
As they last one second but also last one eternity.

life. love. other.

Shopping for pyjamas in Tesco at midnight,
Laughing our way around the deserted aisles,
Because you love me and I love you,
And even one night apart feels like a lifetime.
Or did, once.
Because now every night is apart for a lifetime,
And it's just me wandering the nightwear section
Despite owning all the fucking pyjamas
A grown man could ever need.
(One pair.)

Am I doing it wrong?
I hope not.
For me, it's the little things.

Somer

The high rises were my everything, once.
Beige and grey sarcophagi for a fractured heart.
Smoke, smog, soothing to the soul –
But only because I knew no different.
The clang of the scaffold, beeps of the bus stop.
Brown eyes, white noise. Dark skies, neon joys.
Woolworths, Our Price, Argos, heaven.
South of the river was all I could need.

Then green, green, so very much green.
All it took was a dice roll, a rail track ride.
From mould on walls to moss on trees,
Days spent lazy in daisies and dandelions.
Hikes by the lake, kisses by the moonlight,
Sun-dappled dreams of what might have been –
What might yet be? My every truth is a lie.
All except one. I can never go back.

life. love. other.

You And Me, Kid

This is pure joy.
Sat on a wall,
Sand at our feet,
Sun in the sky,
Sea to one side.

Tide a mile out.
Hot chips. Red dips.
Calm. So much calm.
No more to say.
Just the best day.

Ben Wilson

Train

Flourishing fields I long to roam,
Historic spires and country homes.
Fresh water sprinting into spring,
Perched blackbirds nursing broken wings
As pylons sizzle, stutter, spark
Over taupe trenches spartan, stark.
A troupe of slumber-laden sheep,
And onward, these carriages creep,
No time to take in each pit-stop –
The towns, the roads, the farms, the crops.
The lone constant beyond this view:
The distant sun. The one. The you.

life. love. other.

Ben Wilson

Praise for **One Year Without Social Media** by Ben Wilson

(Amazon review average: 4.7 out of 5)

"It was no surprise to read that Ben is a big fan of Bill Bryson, because I think Bryson would be proud of this book. It's funny, beautifully researched, thoughtful and extremely moving." *****
Chris D, Amazon

"A real-life insight into a young dad's life in our current world: fatherhood, marriage, friendship, work, football, mental health, physical health, expectations about ourselves and those we have placed on us by others. Wow. I loved it." *****
Helen L, Goodreads

"Funny, chatty and it feels like you're talking to a mate down the pub. There are flashes of Bill Bryson, Danny Wallace and Dave Gorman here – charming, witty and very down to earth." *****
Badger Madge, Amazon

"Genuinely not what I expected…
Ben is so nice he's made me less of a misandrist." ****
Nin, Goodreads

"This book was totally, utterly, completely human." *****
Issieatch, Amazon

life. love. other.

Also by the author

Non-fiction:
One Year Without Social Media

Video Gaming:
Next Level Games Review 2023

Social Media

Instagram: @benjiwilson79
Pinterest: @benwilsonpoetry
Threads: @benjiwilson79
TikTok: @benwilson7503
Twitter: @BenjiWilson
YouTube: @rainstoppedplaymusic8617

Acknowledgements

Thanks to Matt Elliott, Kate Hammond, Andrew Leung, Melanie Marshall, Sarah Montrose, Chloe Newport, Sarah-May Rogers, Rowena Smith and Amelia Welham.

Printed in Great Britain
by Amazon